SINGLE, NOT DEAD

Brandy Lucas

LUKE LEGACY
PUBLICATIONS

SINGLE, NOT DEAD

To Alexander & Sheila Lucas, I hope to make you proud.

God, more of you, less of me.

Acknowledgements

Thank you, God for putting this message on heart! My prayer is that your presence is in my words and that it blesses someone. Amen!

To my loving mother, Sheila, thanks for your love and support. You are a blessing in my life. To my father, Luke, resting in heaven, thanks for this beautiful gift of writing you gave me and I hope you're smiling down on me.

To my Spiritual Chicks, thanks for your love and guidance. God brought you in my life to bring me closer to him and glory to his name. To my prayer warriors, mentors, and inspirations, thanks for all the love and prayers that you give me.

To my family and friends, and friends who have become family, I love you!

To every woman out there, God made you a work of art, you are strong and you are beautiful!

Love Always,

Brandy

Table of Contents

INTRODUCTION

YOU'RE SINGLE, NOT DEAD

Okay, so you know how it goes. You're at the family reunion minding your own business enjoying family, music and good food, when your sweet little granny comes up to you and says, "Hey baby, have you gotten married and had any kids yet?" Can you say, mood killer?! I get irritated every time I hear that question. In your head you say to yourself, *Listen granny, did you receive an invitation in the mail announcing my engagement and inviting you to my wedding? Did you get a cute little postcard with a stork carrying a baby inviting you to my baby shower?* Instead of sarcastically responding, you simply smile and shake your head no. You're still not married and you still don't have any children. You think that you can move on from this line of questions until she twists her face up and hits

1

you with, "Well what are you waiting for?" Again, you think to yourself: *Well first, I'm waiting for God to stop sending me people that test my patience, but that's neither here nor there.* If you're anything like me you're still holding on to that smile, but it's now through gritted teeth.

Maybe this is only my life, but if you have reached the age of 30 plus and are not married or in a serious relationship, I'm sure you can relate on some level. Hopefully, you are in the category of women who don't care that they're still single. You're enjoying life to the fullest and being single doesn't define you or make your life less fulfilled. If you are one of those awesome single women, God bless you; I praise you and that's my ultimate goal for myself and every single woman out there. I hope by the end of this book every single woman walks off into the sunset, living her life like it's golden with her head held high, accomplishing goal after goal, with no fear of the future. Until then, many of us ladies—including myself——have some work to do before we get to that happy place.

In China, a single woman over the age of 30 is called a 'leftover woman.' The term leftover woman is used as if she is less desirable or a picked over entrée left in the refrigerator. In a society where single people now outnumber married couples, and about 2 out of 7 people actually live alone, you would think such stigmas wouldn't still exist. I realize that when the statistics say single, they mean not legally married. As we know in this generation, we have all types of non-traditional families; anywhere from same sex couples, to the unmarried couples who call each other "wifey" and "hubby." For the purpose of this book, when I speak of single people, I am referring to a class of people, especially women, who are not married or in a committed exclusive relationship.

When you have been a bridesmaid in several weddings, you start to feel the symptoms of the 'single disease.' After your fifth wedding and seventh baby shower, you start to panic—well at least I did. You start hitting those milestone birthdays and then you enter the 'dirty thirties' and for the first time you hear it. That clock starts ticking; tick, tick, tick. For every wedding invite that comes in the mail, for every friend that asks for you to be in their wedding, for every engagement and anniversary party you get invited to, that noise gets louder. Tick, tick, tick. Your friends tell you to be open, so you go from online dating, to speed dating, to blind dating, to giving your mother's co-worker's husband's nephew Daquan a chance, and the outcome is still the same. Nothing works, you're still single and the disease is spreading. You ask God, Why? What's the hold up? Why hasn't He sent 'the one'? You've read all the books and prayed all the nights—and still crickets. What's the cure for this single's disease? How do you get rid of these symptoms of lonely nights and yearning for that husband, 2.5 kids, and a white picket fence? Whatever your fairytale is, there is a cure to your single disease.

You cure the single disease by realizing, it's not a disease. We are not sick or dead, we just happen to be single for a season. Our season may be a little longer than some, but this too shall pass. We're not dead, we don't have a disease. Being single is just one thing that describes you. It doesn't define you as a person. I don't care if you're 25, 35, or 45, if you're still single just take a deep breath and relax. You're not cursed or being punished, it's as simple as, it is not your time for whatever reason or reasons. Embracing this season doesn't mean convincing yourself that being single is the best life to have and denying the desires of your heart. Embracing your season of singleness is acknowledging that yes you want a relationship, but in the meantime, you will continue working on being the best version of yourself. It's about finding happiness and peace in your now. Embracing your season means healing old wounds, forgiving yourself for past mistakes and stepping into your purpose. It's having faith and not fear of what your future brings. In the upcoming chapters, I challenge myself and all the single ladies out there to grow and improve in all areas of our lives.

Let me be clear on what this book is not. This book is *not* a book telling you how to get a man. Clearly, I don't have the answers for you there. There tons of 'experts' out there that will teach you different tips and tricks to get the attention of a man. This book is not about why you don't have man or why you're still single. Lastly, this book is not coming from an expert who can fix your life with a simple rhetoric or cliché quotes. It's coming from a woman who wants to encourage other women like myself. I give advice that I've learned to take or am starting to understand. You are single; not dead, not less than, not half a person and not deficient. Your worth is not determined by being in a relationship. My goal for every single woman out there for us to all become confident and secure in who we are as ladies so we don't spend our days and nights looking for another person to complete us. Meeting someone will be a cherry on top of the life we've learned to live in abundance. I hope you will join me in this movement and on this journey to the realization that you're SINGLE, not DEAD!

JOURNALING TOPICS

1. How do family and friends make you feel about being single?

2. Do you feel any outside pressures to be in a relationship or marry?

3. If you answered yes to question 2, how do you react to such pressures?

"We cannot think of being acceptable

to others until we have first proven

acceptable to ourselves."

~ Malcom X

CHAPTER 1

WHY DO YOU WANT TO GET MARRIED?

We had a guest speaker one night in Bible study class and he spoke about the Proverbs 31 woman, which led to interesting dialogue. The guest speaker asked the class full of women how many of us were single. Of course, I raised both my hands and feet just in case there was a single man around that needed to know it was real. After posing the question to the group, the teacher looked directly at me and asked, "Brandy do you want to get married?" "Of course," I quickly responded.

"Why? Why do you want to get married?" He asked.

I froze for a moment. *Why do I want to get married?* I retorted with the first thing that came to my mind, "I want to be a wife and mother." *There, that's why;* I thought to myself. But then, he had the nerve to hit me with another why.

"Ok you want to be a wife and a mother, but why?" Everyone stared at me, waiting for my reply. I went blank. Crickets started playing in my mind. Think girl, think! *Why do you want to be a wife and a mother?* I couldn't come up with one response. The speaker moved on with his lesson and I was left sitting there with egg on my face, trying to understand how such simple question had stumped me. I had complained for years about being single; eager to say "I Do". Now that I was tasked with a simple question, I couldn't verbalize why I wanted to get married. I couldn't concentrate the rest of the class. My mind kept going back to that question. I decided on my drive home, that night that I was going to get to the bottom of that question. I turned on some Sade, grabbed a notebook and pen, and told myself that before bed, I owed myself a list of at least five reasons why I wanted to get married. It took me all of five minutes to construct my thoughts. My cute little list was the following:

- Companionship

- Have someone to build an empire with

- Have and raise Godly children who will have a positive impact on society

- Produce a family to leave a legacy to

- To inspire and mentor other couples

Boom! I said to myself; *See girl, you're not crazy. You know why you want to get married.* After I wrote that list, something in my spirit kept nagging at me. I felt like if that pen and notebook could talk, they would tell me I was a lie and the truth wasn't in me. This list sounded great, like I got it out of an article in Essence Magazine, and knowing me I probably did. That list ate at me. It wasn't my truth, it didn't tell my story; it hid my pain.

I can write this book about embracing your singleness as a woman pretending to have it all together. Hiding behind beautiful words to show that I'm an expert on all things covered. I can give advice and preach as if I have all the answers to life's riddles. Or I can be completely transparent, open and honest about my insecurities and flaws in order for growth to take place. I've read enough self-help books, articles, and positive quotes to pretend like I have it all together, but unless I'm auditioning for a movie role, acting won't build my character. After coming clean with myself, I decided that I wanted to write this book not as a self-help expert, but as a real single woman sharing her trials, tribulations, triumphs, and growth as I journey to becoming the best version of myself.

So, after hesitation and reflection, I re-wrote my list of reasons why I want to get married.

- Cure my loneliness

- Everyone I know is married! What is wrong with me?

- Overcome the Spirit of Rejection within

- Looking for someone to make me happy/complete me

- I'm not getting any younger

Ouch! They say the truth hurts, but it will also set you free. Yes, it's true that I want the things from my first, cute little list, too. But deep down, my second list is a more accurate and honest assessment of my motivation to be a Mrs., and my past contempt for the single life. I had to look myself in the mirror and be honest that there are some things I need to work on within myself. There are some insecurities that I must address before stepping into a lifetime commitment with another person. I'm sure we all have hang ups and things that we could improve upon and work through no matter how confident and 'together' we are, but when you are looking for a relationship, person, or thing to 'fix you', then it's time to start a re-evaluation of yourself.

My second list may not be a representation of the majority of single women's motivation to get married, but I think enough single women can relate to at least one of the items off my honest-reasons-for-wanting-to-be-married-list. As I explain the items from my list, if you haven't already, do some self-reflection and think about the honest reasons you yourself no longer want to be single.

Cure My Loneliness

When you get to the root of it, a feeling of loneliness has little to do with people in your life. You could be in a room full of people you know and love and still feel lonely. You can go to bed next to your spouse or significant other and still feel loneliness or the reverse could be that you are alone and don't feel a sense of loneliness. Loneliness is a feeling within, and it's your own perception of your social circumstances. Since loneliness is a personal perception, people and relationships can never be a long-term cure, it will only mask the underlying issue temporarily. Seeking people to cure your loneliness is like taking a pain killer after surgery, it will numb the pain for a few hours, but eventually it will wear off and the pain will return. Yet, no matter how secure you are as a single woman, everyone wants companionship. We are social beings, so desiring healthy companionship is human nature.

When I speak of looking for someone to cure loneliness, I'm speaking of looking for someone to fill a void in your life. Outside of mental health issues, many people that feel a strong sense of loneliness believe that a relationship will cure it. When in reality the loneliness is actually boredom kicking in from not living or understanding your purpose and learning what makes you truly fulfilled. A relationship will give you something or *someone* to do, but it will never fill the void of not learning and understanding your purpose or knowing who you truly are.

Everyone I Know is Married, What's Wrong with Me?

I was supposed to be married in my late 20s, and by now have 2.5 kids and a house with a white picket fence, right? That's what I always envisioned with my childhood best friend as we went through JC Penney catalogs and mapped out how we would decorate our homes. I picked out names for my future kids and already had bridesmaids selected for my wedding day. All my favorite books and television shows gave into my fantasy of how my life would pan out. Fast forward to the real world, and all my friends one by one became Mrs. as I'm stuck at their wedding receptions fighting and throwing elbows trying to catch the bouquets they throw like a NFL wide receiver. How did I end up here? I'm thirty plus; no husband, no man, or prospects. What's wrong with me? I have spent most of my life comparing my life to other people's highlight reels. I've allowed society's standards and norms to define me and diminish my own individuality. I've constantly sought approval and fed off validation. I've constantly lied to myself that I was ready for love when I wasn't even ready to love myself.

Everything happens in God's timing for reasons that we are not meant to understand. He sees the finished picture while we only see one piece at a time. If everyone in your inner circle is married, congratulations for them.

17

Your day will too come. If you are a single woman and you've ever asked yourself what is wrong with you in relation to why you are still single, you are wasting time asking that question. Instead, focus on living a life of abundance, living in your purpose, and continuously growing into the best version of yourself.

You Chose Me, I No Longer Feel Rejected

The spirit of rejection is poison to your soul. It takes one small incident to happen in your life and self-doubt can spread like a cancer. The spirit of rejection began to take root in me at a very early age. I struggled with my weight most of my life and I remember as young as elementary school feeling less beautiful and less attractive than the other girls in my school. Once I started to become interested in boys, the spirit of rejection was able to fester and grow. I felt like none of the boys I was interested in were interested in me. Crush after crush from elementary throughout college, was a self-fulfilling prophecy, and the spirit of rejection and feeling inadequacy increased. Eventually, I began to believe every negative thing about myself; I was too overweight, my teeth, my hair, the way I dressed, the way I talked, were all reasons why these guys didn't find me attractive. I became the friend who held the purses while her friends danced the night away on the dance floor. I became the introvert who preferred a Saturday night home alone, curled up with a romance book reading about women I wanted to emulate and men I wanted to attract, rather than to going out into the real world.

For many years, I allowed the feeling of rejection to tear me down and make me feel unworthy. I believed that only validation could cure rejection. Every compliment I received, every supportive Facebook comment, every Instagram like, every date, gave me the illusion that I was defeating that spirit of rejection. It wasn't until I decided to commit my life to God, ignore the negative things that I was saying about myself and open up to the things He said about me, that I started to repel my spirit of rejection. The battle is not won yet, but I'm fighting. What I've come to learn is that validation and approval will never defeat your battle with feeling rejected. Learning to love the parts of you that are not celebrated, not needing to follow the trends, embracing the things that make you unique, even if the masses think it's weird, following your life passions, even if they are unconventional, is how you begin to defeat the feeling of rejection. Remind yourself every day that validation is for parking only and doesn't apply to your life. If you have issues with the spirit of rejection or constantly seeking approval to feel validated, a marriage or relationship won't fix those issues. It will only expose them.

Marry Me and Make Me Happy

I get it; a lot of things that are important functions in our lives come in pairs. We have our eyes, ears, hands, boobs, passport photos from CVS, windshield wipers, kidneys and more. Those things must function in pairs; you on the other hand do not. You function just fine as a single entity. You are not missing half of yourself, just because you are single. There is no other half out there for you. God gave you everything you need to operate, you are already complete. This isn't an anti-relationship statement or propaganda to prepare you to be alone forever. I'm simply stating that because you're single, doesn't mean you're decaying on life support waiting for your mate like someone waiting for a needed organ. I understand, you're the odd man out on couples' trips and dinners, you leave the plus one section empty on invites, and you snuggle up with your favorite pillow at night instead of a warm body — well let me speak for myself.

Many of us long to someday be married with children or at least have a committed relationship that lasts longer than a romantic comedy. There is absolutely nothing wrong with that. Pray for it, envision it, speak it into existence, and prepare for it as you do anything else you want. The right person can come along and enhance your life to a point where you couldn't imagine life without them. They make you happier when you are with them and your good times with them heavily outweigh the bad. I think this is a more realistic expectation for a partner instead of expecting them to complete you and be the sole reason for your joy.

I'm Not Getting Any Younger

Single women often feel pressured to get married in our society because of age. It makes sense for some single women, especially one without children to feel some form of panic. As women enter their mid to late thirties, they're often aware that their fertility is decreasing. Doctors often automatically label pregnant woman over the age of 35 as high-risk. On top of pressures of bearing children, your thirties and forties introduce you to your first gray hair(s) that line on your face that wasn't there two years, or a stubborn ten pounds after vacation that isn't as easy to get rid of as it was ten years ago. On the other hand the cool thing about getting older is that you're wiser than your younger self hopefully. With wisdom comes maturity and with maturity comes growth. We are a part of new generation, where statistically, many women are starting families later than previous generations. If you haven't fulfilled things that you have hoped to accomplished or been places you said you would visit, don't allow the fact that you're maturing be the main reason you want to be married. Your life is supposed to progress on your own time table, not your sister's, your best friend, or society's expectations.

JOURNALING TOPICS

1. Do you want to get married?

2. If you answered yes, why do you think you want to get married?

3. Honestly speaking, are there any personal insecurities that you believe a relationship or marriage will cure?

"And you shall love the Lord your God with all your heart and with all your soul and with all your mind and with all your strength."

Mark 12:30 (NLT)

CHAPTER 2

FALL IN LOVE WITH GOD FIRST

By definition, I've been saved for most of my life. I've always had a relationship with God and accepted Jesus Christ as my Lord and savior. About a year before writing this book, I decided that I wanted to live my life for God. I decided that I wanted to spend time getting to know his word and promises for my life. If you're a non-believer, you may have a hard relating to much of the advice throughout this book. This is not a religious book, but it is a book encouraging single women to work on being the best version of themselves while embracing the season they're in. It's my belief that in order to accomplish this you need the Father, Son and Holy Spirit. Much of the advice, testimonies, and encouragement brought forth in this book are rooted in Godly advice I received from a believer or mentor, getting to know God through His word, or something I feel God was put on my heart. My faith has dramatically reduced my anxiety and depression about my circumstances and allowed me peace for whatever the future holds for me. This is where I get my strength from. Growing closer to God opens up a type of peace that is unlike any other peace you can give yourself. If you seek Him and pray to Him for it, his peace can keep your mind and heart.

If you have been unwillingly single for a while, you may find yourself questioning God's timing and reasoning. What is His purpose in not introducing you to the right person yet? If you look at a completed puzzle, it has hundreds sometimes thousands of pieces that come together to make it. Once the puzzle is put together you can see how all the pieces fit together to make this complete picture. That's how our lives are, we get little pieces of the puzzle, but God's already sees the completed puzzle. He knows how and when each thing in your life will come together. Do you know how many things you would mess up if God revealed it to you too early? What if He revealed a plan that you didn't agree with at the time too early? He has a plan for your life, will you trust him? Will you trust Him even if the plan is not aligned with what you think is best for your life or what you want for your life? How do you fall in love with the heavenly father? Make sure your first love and priority is God.

To Love Him, Is To Know Him

What if a stranger pulled up in a car next to you and said, "Come follow me, I have something amazing in store for you. The catch is you only can receive it if you trust and follow me." Since we were kids, most of us have been programmed not to trust in people or things we don't know.

If you don't trust and follow God, it could be because he is a stranger to you. You can't trust something you don't know. You may have heard of God, you may go to church, you may pray to Him, but if you don't *know* him, he is a stranger to you. You only know of him from what you've been told. You have to know him for yourself. You may say you love God, but really, you just know you should or were told you should. You can't rely on religion or what your pastor says, or what your parents said about him, or by like a few bible scriptures that someone posted on social media. You must seek Him for yourself to learn the promises He has for you.

Some people will tell you in order to get to know him, you must learn his word. I agree to a certain extent, but I personally found that seeking Him first through prayer is what helps to develop a stronger relationship with Him. Pray to Him to change to your heart and your mind. Ask Him to give you a closer relationship with Him and let Him know you're interested in getting to know Him better. Pray that prayer as long as it takes, and you will see Him bring people into your life whose sole purpose is to bring you closer to Him.

Getting That Word

I wasn't a big fan of sitting around reading the Bible. It seemed extra boring, and the King James Version with all that giveth and taketh language was confusing, not relatable, and with my short attention span I would read one sentence and be put the Bible right back down and pick up a trashy romance novel instead. Thank God for my Bible study group; they made learning the bible fun by covering different topics that were relatable for me. If you're struggling with your relationship with Christ or new to your walk, I wouldn't recommend just opening the bible and reading without guidance. Pray for guidance and use trial and error to figure out what works better for your learning style. Try different versions of the Bible to see which wording you understand best. If you're tech savvy, download a Bible app that lets you quickly switch between different versions for better understanding. Most Bible Apps have different learning plans that will help you understand the word as well. If you hate reading, try an audio version of the Bible. If you're new to learning the

Bible, I recommend starting with the books of the Bible that focus on Jesus' gift of salvation to the world such as Luke, Matthew or John.

Focus on His Love, Not Rules

A spiritual mentor once gave me great advice when she said, "First understand that God is love, and then begin to pray that He brings you closer to Him. As you get to know God, how He sees you, the promises He has for your life through his word, and the love He has for you, you will begin to change and live the life He wants you to live because you love Him and you want to please Him—not because the Bible tells you so. This is one of the best pieces of advice I have received since I began my walk. The more I read His word, the more I surrounded myself with people who loved God, and the more I understood that I was loved, my lifestyle begin to change. Some of my desires begin to change. When God began to reveal to me that he created my body as a temple, I didn't want to give it to just anyone. When God revealed to me how precious he made the woman, I stop desiring to listen to music that degraded womanhood and didn't uplift me. I started rejecting drama and desired more positivity. Once I strengthened my prayers, the Holy Spirit inside of me started to guide me on how to live my life.

Find a Spiritual Circle or Mentor

I've written much about the positive sides of deciding to live a life ordained by God, but I want to make clear that the walk will not be easy. We live in a sinful world where it's the enemy's job to rob of us our joy, interrupt our purpose and pull us away from God. This walk can get lonely, because giving your life to the Lord, means becoming a new being. The old you must die to give birth to the new person you will need to become. You need people in your life who have already built a strong relationship in Christ that will encourage you to grow closer to God. When your faith wavers and you are in the middle of a spiritual warfare, you need spiritual warriors to stand with you, pray for you and encourage you during those difficult times, and lovingly hold you accountable. Whether you join a faith based church that you have a fellowship with or join a group of believers, you need spiritual warriors to have your back.

Seek Him Daily

What's the first thing you do when you get up in the morning before your foot touches the ground? Do you wake up and hit the ground running? Do you check your emails, social media, or missed text messages? Think of a time when you were madly in love or lust with someone. Were they the first thing on your mind when you woke up? Did you send them a good morning text? Were you anticipating their call or text? How many times a week did you see them or communicate with them?

Does God receive the same courtship you extend to someone you're madly in love with? I know I'm guilty of not putting God first throughout my day. I recently stopped the bad habit of grabbing my phone and heading straight to social media when I wake up in the morning. I used to catch up on all the social media I missed overnight, then I would click on the Bible app and read a scripture or two, or follow whatever Bible plan I started. After that, I would say *oh yeah, God thanks for waking me up this morning* and off I would go to the hustle and bustle of the world without a second thought of Him until I came home and said my nightly prayers. Ladies, imagine being in a relationship with someone who takes five minutes out of 24 hours to spend time and communicate with you and you only see them on Sundays. I don't know about you, but I would be convinced that I was some side chick and he was married or in another relationship.

Oftentimes we treat God like a genie that we come to when we need a wish granted or a side piece that we only can carve out a few minutes of our day for because we are married to our other Gods: money, work or family. I think we're all guilty of this at some point in our walk. Treat God like the love of your life. Praise and thank Him before your feet touché the floor, ask Him to guide you throughout the day, pray for Him to strengthen your faith, ask Him how you can bring Him glory daily. Pray that He changes your heart and mind so that your desire to please Him is constant.

Find Your Purpose

I think the most important thing a woman can do whether she is single or married, besides developing and strengthening her relationship with God, is to determine her purpose. Think about why you are here and what your purpose is. What makes you unique and what are you contributing to society? Beginning to walk and live in that purpose is gratification like no other. For many years I suffered from depression, feeling inadequate, low self-esteem, and wondering if I could ever be happy. I thought that more money would make me happy, or being in a relationship, losing weight, or maybe even a change of scenery. I eventually made more money, lost weight, moved to a different city, traveled, and I still couldn't shake that feeling of emptiness or unhappiness in my life. It wasn't until I started building a stronger relationship with God that I saw myself differently and began to overcome some of my demons.

When I started my publishing company and my writing transitioned from being a hobby to a business, I began to envision a life where I could mentor and encourage people with my words. I have begun to see how God wants to use me. Not to say that I've reached my destination or I have it all figured out, but since I've begun to understand my purpose, my life and what I feel about it has changed for the better. When you begin to understand what you are called to do and begin to walk in your purpose, you are less likely to be jealous or envious of other people because you know what God has for you is uniquely yours. God has a plan for you and if you have started to live in your purpose continue to grow and don't let obstacles or fear hold you back. If you haven't discovered your purpose, begin to seek God's guidance and he will reveal the calling he has on your life.

Let Him Transform You

I'm a woman with a testimony of how God's love has changed me. That doesn't mean that I don't have bad days, and my faith doesn't waver, or that my circumstances don't sometimes steal my joy, but my mind always comes back to him and he guides me home. I use to sit and bathe in pity, let depression keep me in the house for days, let jealousy and envy eat me up inside like a cancer. Now I'm heavily medicated with His word. Without realizing it, He's been slowly changing my heart and mind. It was slow minor changes, I pray more, I'm thankful for little things that I use to complain about, I try to encourage people, and I look for positive things in my storms. Little by little he is changing me.

If you do have a prayer life, start to look at what you're praying for. Ask Him to change your perspective of your circumstances instead of changing the circumstances. Ask Him for peace during the situation instead of changing it. Asking Him to change your situation is not always the best prayer, not because He can't change your circumstances, but because He won't if it's not a part of His complete plan for your life. He can see the bigger picture while we can only see what we've been through and what we are going through. Everything has a purpose, because we don't know His purpose doesn't negate that He is wise and loving. It simply means we don't understand.

God wants to be the gateway of your peace and happiness. He wants you fall in love with him as He is with you. If you think that a man will complete you) and not God, that's upsetting to Him. Exodus 34:14 tells us God is jealous when we worship something above him. Don't worship a life that you think you want or need. Telling God that you want to get to know Him and grow closer to him will be like music to his ears. He will begin to reveal himself to you and show you ways to get close to him. Then ask that he change your heart, mind and desires.

You remember your parents ever saying you don't understand now but you will when you get older or when you have kids of your own, you will understand? That was their way of saying, "I love you and I know what's best for you even if you don't understand it or agree with it. You're too immature to understand that this is what has to be done to protect you." Just as your parents said that to you in their own way, God is saying the same thing to us. He knows it frustrates us and we get mad and annoyed. And just like your parents, it's not that He doesn't care that you're hurt or upset, it's that He knows He is doing what's best for you and Him doing what's best for you is more important than making you happy in that moment. Understand that God doing what's best for you can save your life and protect you from harm. So, stop throwing a tantrum like your teenage self when your mom told you that you couldn't go somewhere, or stay out late, or wear a certain outfit, and trust that you are being covered and loved. Seek His kingdom first and let Him guide your path. You'll understand when you get older!

JOURNALING TOPICS

1. Is your relationship with God a priority in your life?

2. Is it a goal of yours to put God first in your life?

3. If you answered yes to number two, list three things you will do differently to grow spiritually.

"We have to confront ourselves. Do we like what we see in the mirror? And according to our light, according to our understanding, according to our courage, we will have to say yea or nay—and rise."

~Maya Angelou

CHAPTER 3

WORK ON YOU

Every Tuesday, I meet with a lovely group of Godly women called, Spiritual Chicks. It's a Bible study group led by some awesome Godly women who bring ladies together to fellowship with one another and bring them closer to God. We discuss real issues that women deal with on their spiritual walk. The group of ladies has had a tremendous impact on my life and my walk with God. One particular Tuesday, we watched a video of a popular sermon done by a well-known female televangelist.

Before I go into the video and how it changed my perspective and the direction of this book, let me first tell you my mindset before someone hit play on the television to show this video. If you would have asked me if I was ready to be in a relationship or be a wife and mother, I would have been offended by the question. Am I ready to be in a relationship? Of course, I am! I'm beyond ready. I've read every relationship book, I give great relationship advice to my girlfriends, I'm growing closer to God, and I go to church on Sundays and Bible study twice a week. I pay my tithes and I pray every night; I even pray for my future husband. I post deep quotes and Bible verses on Instagram. I really believed that the reason God hadn't sent me a husband yet because whoever he is was the one not ready yet, not me. It couldn't possibly me who was not ready.

From the title, I was expecting the video to be about why single women should remain abstinent and to a certain degree it was about that, but it went deeper. I was prepared to hear about how we as single women should be abstinent and wait for marriage. If that was the only message, I could have handled that one. I sat on the couch, got comfortable and prepared to yell out a few "Amens" and "Uhmm hmmms" along with a couple of "Preach," then go home feeling good about myself. Twenty minutes into the video, I was pissed beyond belief. The messenger started preaching and I got offended as if she said that the message was specifically for me, Brandy Lucas. She spoke about all this baggage I was carrying, my self-esteem, I didn't own any property, my credit score was low, I didn't have any money saved, and I was waiting on a man to build me up instead of relying on God. When she finished preaching, I thought, *No she didn't go in on me like that.* I know a lot of women who are married who don't have it all together, why did she come for me like that?

It struck a nerve with me because everything she talked about was absolutely right. There was a laundry list of things I needed and still need to work on. After I got out of my feelings, the validity of the message set in for me. Why was I so consumed with not having a man, when I should be consumed with getting myself together for me? It was the first time I was honest with myself and admitted that just because I wanted a relationship, didn't mean I was necessarily ready for one.

We will always have things to work on and improve on in our lives. Whether single, married or dating; we all need some work. When you get in a relationship that will hopefully lead to marriage, you want to be a great partner, helper and upgrade to that person, as you would want them to be to you. The two of you should be like a great merger that makes both companies better. That's how a relationship should be, two people coming together and their merger making them a force to reckon with. When you enter a relationship, especially marriage, you want to bring something to the table other than great looks and great sex. Don't get me wrong, I'm sure both of those attributes would be greatly appreciated by your partner, but you should want to offer more than that when joining a team. You should want to be asset and not a liability. When I first typed asset, I starting think about the feminist and strong independent women that would have a problem with that word. I see them now sending me mean tweets stating that they don't have the desire to be someone's property. But when I looked up the word asset, the first definition stated "a useful or valuable thing, *person,* or quality." The synonyms listed for asset were benefit, advantage, blessing, good point, strong point, selling point, strength, virtue, merit, and bonus. On the other hand, when I looked up liability the definition I ran into was, "a person or thing whose presence or behavior is likely to cause embarrassment or put one at a disadvantage." The synonyms listed under liability were hindrance, burden, handicap, nuisance, and inconvenience. I don't know about you but I want to be a blessing to my future husband not an inconvenience. I want to be a bonus not a burden. So I gave you this short vocabulary lesson to say, although you will never be perfect, you will still have issues because you're human, strive to be the best version of yourself that you possibly can. Striving to be the best version of your self will give you confidence in who you are and what you bring to the table in a relationship. Feeling like you're ready for a relationship doesn't always mean that you're ready for a relationship. For the rest of the chapter and book, do some self-reflecting to outline some areas you can improve on for yourself.

JOURNALING TOPICS

1. List three things that you really like about yourself.

2. List three things about yourself that you have control of that you want to improve or change.

3. List one item for each three things you listed that you will do differently to make improvements.

"If you don't value your time, neither will others. Stop giving away your time and talents. Value what you know and start charging for it."

~Kim Garst

CHAPTER 4

GET YOUR BUSINESS IN ORDER

Money is a big part of our lives whether we care to admit it or not. We are always working to get more. People kill, lie, cheat and steal for it. On the other hand, people use it to donate to the poor, bring people closer to God with programs and charities, and provide a stable life for them and their families. Whether you choose to use it for necessity, good, or evil, it comes down to the fact that we need money or some form of currency here on earth. When you think about your finances what are some of your goals? Do you aim to be debt free, if so by what date? How much money do you have saved for an emergency, $1000, 3 months of expenses, 6 months of expenses, or nothing? Do you live pay check to pay check

51

scraping to get by or do you have financial freedom? What does financial freedom look like to you?

Whether it is to save up for a down payment for your home, travel, explore, uncover passions or interests, or a start business, your finances and credit need to be in order to allow you the freedom to do those things. You will need to have some disposable income if you want to live a fulfilling life embracing your singleness.

Financial stability and freedom also allows you to help others by donating to your local church, charitable organizations, children or family with special needs or mission trips. We can't be cheerful givers if we're always thinking about our debt or lack of income. Sometimes it takes money to be a blessing to someone in need or influence a community. Although it doesn't always take money to help people or influence situations, it doesn't hurt.

You don't want to go into a marriage with thousands of dollars in debt, no savings, with the responsibility of the finances falling solely on your partner. You want to be an asset, not a liability. If your credit score is low, then it will affect you both when you're trying to acquire things for your family. Remember, marriage and relationships are like a team where each player helps their teammate to achieve the goals. Just like a card game, you and your partner both get a hand and your goal is to work together with that hand to win the game. If both of you have strong hands, you will be unbeatable, but if one partner has a really great hand, and the other partner has a terrible hand, you can easily lose the game because one partner's hand was so bad it brought the entire team down. Finances are one of the top reasons for divorce, so we want to have our money in order while we are single in case we choose to get married.

Financial gurus like Dr. Boyce Watkins, Dave Ramsey, Suze Orman, or David Bach all offer sage advice that can help you become financially fit. The tips I'm suggesting will help you evaluate your financial goals. Be sure to do your own research for better ways to make your money work for you. Here are a few ideas of ways to improve your finances:

SET A GOAL, MAKE A PLAN

Pick up a spiral notebook and some pens and highlighters. Think about your financial goals. Your goals may include purchasing a home, paying off student loan debt, starting an emergency fund, investing or starting your business. Determine what *your* goals are. Once you've determined what your goals are, write them down. Seeing your goals written down will bring clarity to your situation. If you haven't picked up on it yet, I love lists. While creating your list, be specific as possible about the goals you want to achieve. If saving money is your goal, determine a realistic amount. If you want to pay off your credit card debt, select a date by which you want to achieve this. If you want to start a business, research the start-up costs and how you will fund your venture. After you write out your goals, in the order you want to accomplish them, plan how you will get your goals accomplished. A few of the upcoming tips in this chapter will help you learn on how to tackle some of your financial goals.

BUDGET

I personally hate budgets, but they are a necessary evil; we need them. Every company and business needs a budget to track their expenses and profits. You are your own personal business, so yes you need to write down a budget, not try to calculate it in your head. Write it down! I repeat: *write it down*. Review your last few pay stubs, and then take a look at your recurring bills like utilities, internet, cable, cell phone, mortgage or rent, car insurance, car note, etc., and write the totals down. Don't forget about items that are sometimes overlooked or such as gas and transportation, groceries, gym memberships or tithing. Most importantly, don't forget to write down what you spend on fast food, eating out, and entertainment. The eating out and entertainment part of the budget is the part where most people underestimate how much they spend. There are cool apps that you can download that link to your debit card, showing you how much you've spent in each category. If you're not into technology or paranoid about apps having access to your banking info, get a copy of your financial bank statement. I recommend taking a look at 90 days of your bank statement to get a more accurate picture of how much you have been spending in each category. Don't try to guess. Remember the saying, the truth will set you free.

Write down your income that you bring in every month and subtract the outgoing money from the incoming money. Are you spending less than you bringing in? If the answer is yes, then cool, you get your first gold star. You have some money to put toward your financial goals. If you're spending more than you make, there is a problem with how you handle your finance. The next thing to do is see if you can cut expenses. Perhaps consider reducing your cell phone plan or coverage. I recently saved $100 by switching to a different cell phone provider; the new services sucks, but for $100 in savings I will survive. Ponder on cutting your cable or reduce the amount of channels to save some money. I saved myself about $120 once I got rid of my cable. I kept my internet and I now watch television on streaming devices. You also may consider cutting out an expense gym membership if it you're not consistently working out. Also think about downsizing your apartment or house, or get a roommate. You may have already done these things or be in a financial situation where you don't need to. Either way, make sure you keep a budget. A budget will tell your money what to do and show you where it goes.

TACKLE YOUR DEBT and IMPROVE YOUR CREDIT SCORE

If you are debt free and have a credit score that's in the mid to high 700s or 800s, you get two more gold stars! I salute you on a job well done. For the rest of us who are like myself and still have some work to do to be financially fit, this is our season to get ourselves on point. Tackle your debt head on. I will be completely honest and say in the past I just ignored my debt—especially student loans—as if they would magically disappear. I closed my eyes really tight, waved a magic wand, said "Abracadabra," and to my shock, my debt was still there. You're trying to figure out why you don't get approved for that home loan, or your interest rate is high on your next car. Pull your credit report and know your score. Don't guess based off what it was 2 years ago, or even 6 months ago. Make sure all the items listed on your credit report are accurate and make any necessary disputes. Having a high credit score can save you money on high interest rates when purchasing a home, car or business.

Once you have a good look at your debt, set a plan in motion on how to get rid of it. Many experts differ on this approach. Some will tell you to pay debt off using the snowball effect, where you pay off your smallest debt first and work your way up from there, while others will tell you to tackle your highest debt first. Pick what works for you; plan, execute, and get it done! Give yourself a realistic timeframe to pay off your debt and celebrate the small wins. There are also financial experts that can help you build and repair your credit, but be careful not to get caught in a debt consolidation scam that further damages your credit.

While you're trying to eliminate your debt and improve your credit score, don't fall into the *Keeping up With the Jones* trap. Trying to keep up with other people and what they have is another way to stay in debt. Having to have the latest anything because someone else has it or you want to appear to have more than you actually do, does not benefit your financial stability and actually speaks to a self-esteem issue on your part. Trying to keep with other people or using your possessions to impress people or seek validation shows that you may be covering up some insecurities or making up for an area you feel inadequate in. The saying goes it's better to actually be blessed than to look blessed. Spend your life having money instead of looking like you have money. You don't want to spend your life investing in material things but have failed to invest in your future, invest in your savings, and failed to have discipline in keeping a great credit score.

SAVE AND CUT BACK ON IMPULSE BUYING

We all see those awesome stilettos, cute purses, overpriced make-up or little black dress that we have to have because we have absolutely nothing to wear. I'm guilty of this too; my closet is over flowing with clothes. We live in a consumer society where we smart marketing convince us that we need the latest smart phone, the newest model car, or latest pair of designer shoes. We see it and we want it. We justify it by saying, "I work hard," "I deserve this," or, "I don't work as hard as I do just to pay bills." Constantly having that mindset can cause you to live a debt filled life and shows irresponsibility with your finances. Don't get me wrong, of course you want to treat yourself to nice things especially when you work so hard. The problem comes when you have the mindset of constantly binge purchasing or purchasing unnecessary items when your finances are not in order. The truth is that most of us can't get everything we see. But until that business you started takes off, or you're blessed with an inheritance, or you win the lottery, you will be one of those people where money matters. If you are not one of those people who skipped to the next chapter because their finances are in order, then this is not the season for you to be a consumer. This is the season of cutting back and saving.

Although saving is an easy concept, it can be difficult to put into practice. Many people claim they don't have enough disposable income to save, but often time its lack of planning and discipline that prevents saving. If you have trouble saving, start off with small changes over time and work your way up to larger saving goals. Find ways to cut back on any excess spending into you reach your goals. Here are a few of these tips that can help you get serious about saving:

- Make a yearly realistic savings goal.

- If you have a job that offers 401k, make sure you are at least contributing the employer match

- Open a savings account that is not attached to your checking

- Have a small amount automatically deducted from your payroll check (make sure it's going into a savings that is not attached to your checking)

- Sell old items in your home that you no longer use such as books and clothing online or at a garage sale and put the proceeds in your savings account.

- Put the extra money from your annual raise automatically in your savings account or go up a percent on your 401k contributions.

Cut back on luxury (i.e. nails appointment, massage, dinner with friends) for three months to a year and save that money. Another way to cut back and save some extra cash is to consider your living situation. Maybe a roommate or even moving back home with your parents for 6-24 months may help set you up for financial success. I know that moving back with family or close friends is not the best option but sometimes it's better than the option of remaining a slave to your financial woes.

Priorities are important in every aspect of our lives especially with our money. Remember give more than you borrow, save for a rainy day, and don't let debt consume your finances. Proverbs 22:7 states, "Just as the rich rule the poor, so the borrower is servant to the lender."

MAKE MORE MONEY

Making more money is necessary sometimes to achieve your financial goals. Before you take steps to make more money, try your best to live below your means with the money you already have and once you are introduced to more, stay conservative and don't increase your lifestyle to match your new income. If you remember to write down a budget, prioritize your spending and minimize splurging, you will have more money.

Making more money can encompass a lot of things from starting a new business part time, selling old items, searching for a job that makes more, or walking into your boss office and asking for a raise. My personal choice is starting your own business or side hustle. Entrepreneurship even on a small scale, with minimal or no overhead costs, can be your ticket to financial freedom. At most jobs, no matter how hard you work, you're capped at how much money you can make—especially if you're salary as opposed to hourly. When you make money for yourself, depending on the industry, there is no cap on your salary. Figure out creative ways to use your gifts and talents to produce something profitable. Your passions often offer clues to potential earnings.

Another way to bring in more money is through investments. You can invest your money into stocks and bonds, CDs, Roth IRAs, and or a 401k. You can invest your money into real estate in several ways such as obtaining and renting out a rental property, joining other investors in a real estate investment group, or purchasing a home and flipping it for resale. You can also invest in other people businesses where you get a return on your investment without having to contribute to labor. Spend time online, researching experts and seek out books that will give you creative and smart ways to invest your money.

You can choose other ways to make extra money like picking up a part-time job or if you're hourly picking up extra hours at your full-time job. I only recommend a second job as a temporary fix to alleviate some financial tensions. You want to still have free time to enjoy your life and pursue your passions whatever they may be.

If your savings account is on E for empty and your debt is on F for full, then 'tis the season to make the necessary changes you need to be financially stable and secure. Most recommend that you have at least 6 months of emergency fund saved for a rainy day which can include anything from car repair to roof repairs for your home. You will have to make sacrifices in order to get any results you want in life. Your finances are no exception.

JOURNALING TOPICS

1. List five financial goals you have for yourself in the next 3-5 years.

2. List three behaviors or things that you need to improve or change to hit your financial goals.

3. Commit to one or more of the following: reading one book, listening to a podcast, watching a video, or attending one class in the next 30 days that will help you with your financial goals.

"I am no longer accepting the things I cannot change... I'm changing the things I cannot accept."

~Angela Davis

CHAPTER 5

GET RID OF EMOTIONAL BAGGAGE

Do you remember that Erykah Badu song, "Bag Lady"? The lyrics are simple, but prolific. My favorite one is, "You can't hurry up, 'cause you got too much stuff." That line rings so clear to me because too much baggage will slow you down in life. Reflect on some of the baggage that you may be holding on to. How much dead weight is it adding to your life? I think one of my biggest flaws is I hold onto things good or bad. My best friend once told a story about me in bible study that made me put my head down in shame. The subject focused on forgiveness, and she told the class about how I still held a grudge against a girl that mistreated me in the third grade. I'm sure if I saw this woman today I couldn't even pick her out of a line up for a million dollars. If you've ever hurt me in my life and I don't care how long it was, I can remember it. As we are becoming powerful women who want to achieve great success and happiness in our lives, we have to let go of our baggage, hurt, pain and insecurities. There's no room for love when your life is clogged up with all this stuff from your past. It's too heavy to carry on our backs, it keeps us in shackles and we don't even realize it. It's blocking our blessings and keeping us from our destiny.

Forgiveness

Not granting forgiveness is one of the heaviest bags of emotional trash that you can carry around. Not forgiving someone will actually eat at you and may not even bother a hair on them. Although I struggle with forgiveness, I'm aware that I'm blessed and I haven't experienced traumatic events that are impossible for me to forgive. I realize people suffer extreme disappointment, heartbreak and pain that I can't even imagine. There are women dealing with being molested, raped, abandoned, neglected, beaten, rejected, and mistreated at the hands of people they love and trust. I would be insensitive and shortsighted to compare applying forgiveness in these cases to my trivial beef in the third grade. This is why forgiveness is so important because it frees us from our prison and allows us to begin to heal. It may be a difficult task, but it is a necessary one to push forward. When you don't forgive, you are stuck in the past. You won't progress or grow because you're fixated on this past situation that has wronged you. You stay in a victim mentality that doesn't allow you to be victorious.

When you don't forgive, you give the person who wronged you the power to have control over you. You allow them to steal your joy even if only for a second. No matter how hard it is, how wronged you were, or how long it takes, you need to forgive. Forgive even if you don't receive an apology. Forgive even if the person who wronged you doesn't agree that they wronged you. Forgive them anyway. Pass out forgiveness like Oprah used to pass out gifts on her show. You get forgiveness! You get forgiveness! Everybody gets forgiveness!

The most important reason to forgive is because God forgives you about a million times a day What if God didn't forgive us? That's a pretty scary thought to me. Matthew 6:14 states, "If you forgive those who sin against you, your heavenly Gather will forgive you. But if you refuse to forgive others, your Father will not forgive your sins."

Our Past

Our past can be another piece of baggage that we need to throw away. I believe everybody has something from their past that haunts them. Whether it's daddy issues, fear of rejection, constantly needing validation, or just a negative attitude, it can reflect in you and turn people off. I call it the shoulda-woulda-couldas. If I could have done this I should have done this, if I would have done this my life could be different or better. If this person didn't do this to me, or this didn't happen, I would be here instead of there.

Living in the past is pointless and destructive. You can't go back and save your old self, so live in the present and prepare for the future. You may have done things in the past that you are ashamed or embarrassed about, but that was the old you and you're not the same person you use to be. Ask God for forgiveness, forgive yourself, and move on. Whoever is in your life that won't let you forget your past, forgive and separate yourself from them. Only positive vibes need apply.

Negative People

Negative people usually leave a trail of negative energy in their wake, if you allow it. They can bring down your mood, make you second guess your abilities, and crush your dreams and spirit. If you're already struggling in certain areas such faith, self-esteem, or love, a negative person is not someone you should constantly keep around. Many times, we adopt some of the traits of the people we are closest to. If you see that you're complaining more, have a negative outlook on life, or never have anything good to say, check your inner circle to see the type of people in your life. It may be time to discontinue some relationship and limit others.

You may not think that your baggage is showing, but it's all around you. Whether it's your opinions, or attitude, or the way you treat people, your baggage is with you wherever you go. Remember to pack light, do some spring cleaning in your life and get rid of the baggage.

JOURNALING TOPICS

1. List some emotional baggage that you have from your past.

    a. Who or what caused it?

    b. How long have you held on to it?

    c. What ways will you get rid of your baggage (i.e. therapy, journaling, speaking with the source of the baggage, prayer)?

2. Think of someone that you need to forgive.

    a. What did they do to need your forgiveness?

    b. Write down their name on a separate piece of paper.   Under their name write.   I FORGIVE YOU!

"We're so busy watching out for what's ahead of us that we don't take time to enjoy where we are."

~Bill Waterson

CHAPTER 6

ENJOY YOUR NOW

I don't have any single friends. I have about 5-6 close friends, and they are all married. A few years ago for my 30th birthday, I visited Las Vegas for the first time. At the time, I hadn't traveled much outside of business or family engagements because all of my friends were coupled off and I didn't want to travel as the third wheel. A few of my close friends and family members suggested that I do something special for my 30th, so I invited everyone I knew—parents, friends, aunts, and uncles—on this trip. When it was time to actually go, only myself and two other couples actually went. The thought of going on my first real trip being surrounded by couples didn't sound like my idea of a good time at all. My apprehension was increased by the fact that I was turning 30 with no man, no husband and no prospects. My four friends and I had already paid for our trip, so I couldn't back out.

To make this long story short, I got there and had one of the best times of my life. The five of us really enjoyed ourselves and I didn't care that I was solo. I was too busy enjoying myself to feel sorry for myself. I was enjoying my life. My friends that accompanied me couldn't believe it was my first big trip. I realized that I had put off traveling all these years because I didn't want to travel alone or with my coupled friends. How crazy is that thought process? After the Vegas trip, the five of us planned a tripped to Mexico that was even better than Las Vegas. In Mexico, I knocked about three items off my bucket list, all in one trip. My next few trips that followed were with my married friends and we have future trips planned. Yes, I will be the odd man out, but I don't care. I'm blessed to have the group of friends that I have and I wouldn't trade them for the world.

Why miss out on seeing the world because you're not attached to someone? Life will never be perfect and it will never go according to plan. You have to seize the moment and choose to be happy. Even if you're not where you want to be, find things you like about the season you're in. Don't miss out on opportunities you may never get again just because you don't have a plus one.

My two god-sisters, who are happily married with children, and I get together sometimes for what we call, "sister time." It's usually at the eldest's home, but every once in a while we have it at my place. They always joke about how peaceful my home is without kids or a husband running up to me screaming, *Mommy this* and *Honey that*, and how I have an unlimited amount of beauty products that haven't been tampered with or destroyed by children. I laugh when they talk about how my toilet seat is always down and I have an unlimited supply of paper towel (my one sister has some control issues with paper towel). Now would my sisters trade my life for theirs? Absolutely not, they love their husbands and kids and wouldn't trade them for the world—at least not on most days.

There are definitely perks to being single. I get to be selfish and think about my needs and what makes me happy. When I'm tired and I want to sleep after a long day of work I come home to a peaceful house. Some days I'm a neat freak with not one thing out a place, and other days I come home, get butt naked in the middle of the living room—my clothes thrown across the couch. No judgment please. I don't know why I do it, I just do because I can, I guess. There is no one to come home and be irritated with me that I was too lazy to drop my pants in the dirty clothes hamper instead of leaving them on the couch. I know how to cook because my mother forced me to learn but I'm usually not in the mood to cook. Most of the time I grab something on the go, bum dinner off my mom, pop in a TV dinner, or invite myself to dinner over one of my friend's house. No husband or kids at home to ask what's for dinner. I cook when I want and I pretty much do what I want because I don't answer to anyone. When I see something cute, if I have the money for it, I buy it. Let's be honest, sometimes I don't have the money and I still buy it. Hey, I'm still a work in progress. If I spend my money on something stupid, it doesn't cause an argument between anyone but the devil on my left shoulder and the angel on right. I worry about myself and I answer to myself.

Would I trade my life of throwing my clothes where I want, spending money without permission, no kids using up my beauty products, or no husband leaving the toilet seat up for a husband, two kids, a dog, and a house with a white picket fence? Yes, in a heartbeat, but for now, I'm enjoying things that are great about being single. When you get married, you become one with another human being and become a team. The two of you will have to compromise, come to agreement about everything from finances to how you will go about raising your children. As exciting as all that is, it's also scary. Everything is no longer all about you and what you want. It now becomes what's best for the family.

Advance in Your Career

Being single without children is an opportune time to be ambitious and go after everything you want career wise. Whatever advancing in your career looks like, when you are solo there are less distractions and responsibilities that will hold you back or slow you down. If you decide to further your education, you can devote your time to school or school and work depending on your circumstances. People who are married or married with children have to consider the needs of others. Yes, an attached person can go back to school or receive additional education to further their career, but it's usually a lot harder. You sacrifice quality time with your immediate family in order to achieve your goal.

Even in cases where you advance your career without going to school, sometimes it takes late nights or staying past your scheduled time to get all the necessary things done to shine for the powers that be. Take this time as a single person to put in the extra time and effort you need in order to advance to the next level. Focus on a goal and go after it.

Entrepreneurship/ Business

Entrepreneurs hold a special place in my heart. I have a great deal of respect for a person who decides to live outside the status quo and create their own opportunities. Starting and operating your own business is no easy task. For most entrepreneurs, the beginning phases of a new business can be extremely intense and time consuming. Often times small business owners, due to financial obligations, are starting their new businesses while still working full-time or part-time for someone else. If you want to start a business, or invest in different avenues, the best time to do it is when you're single. You don't have to get another person on board with your vision. In many cases, your success or failure only affects you. You can put in late nights without feeling guilty about missing kids' dance recitals or date night with your spouse. This is the time to pursue your dreams and passions and go after the things you've always wanted.

Take Once in a Lifetime Chances and Opportunities

If you've always wanted to move to Paris, travel the world, or bet it all on black, the time to do it is now. If tomorrow you decided that you wanted to quit your job, sell everything you owned and spend the year traveling all around the world, today would be the day to do it. I'm not encouraging you to quit your job without a financial plan, but you could if you wanted to. You could invest your life savings into a dream; you could move from your small town to New York City, you could spend two months on that mission trip in Africa, or whatever else you wanted to do in this world. If you've always wanted to move to Los Angeles to see if you have what it takes to be a star in

Hollywood, now is the time to take that risk. Your dreams don't have necessary die when you get married and have a family, but you have to think about how your decisions will affect your family and loved ones. Take a moment and think about some items on your bucket list. Think about things you always wanted to do in life but haven't had a chance to experience yet. Start getting those items checked off your list. Life is too short for regret. I realize that it will take time to do everything, but you can make a plan to start living your life as if there's no tomorrow. Life can be hard so you have to find little pieces of heaven while you're here on earth. Even if for a brief moment, stop and enjoy the life you have, God only gives you one to live.

Be Grateful for your Support System

I talk about being single throughout this book, but I would be remiss if I didn't mention my great support system. I have so many people in my life that encourage me in my singleness. I have so many people that pray for my peace, spirit and mind. I have loving people who tell me not to worry that I haven't found someone or that I'm not married yet. I have happily married friends that tell me that God has something amazing for me so trust him. I don't have a mother who tells me how much she wants grandkids after asking me when I am going to meet someone, every time she sees me. I have a mother who encourages me to chase after my dreams, go travel, work on myself and love myself. I have these amazing people in my life who say come out with us, who cares if you're single, you're our family. They don't make me feel like a third wheel; they make me feel loved. Does their love replace a strong, chiseled husband snuggled up close to me to keep me warm at night? Uhmmm, no, but their love is important to me. It's great to be genuinely loved and supported in any type of relationship. Don't take for granted the loved ones in the trenches with you. The support system that I'm referring to should want to see you happy at any stage of your life.

Network with People like You

Hanging out with a group of cool, mature, well-rounded, single women may do you good. You may feel more comfortable with a group of people who understand what you go through as a single woman. If you happen to meet someone who is single like you and you guys hit it off, try networking with them. You may be lucky to find a group of single friends that are looking for the same things you are. Even if you have a great support system, sometimes it's great to step out of that comfort zone and meet new people. It's important to surround yourself with positive people who encourage you to live a meaningful life.

JOURNALING TOPICS

1. List three perks of being single.

2. List three things that you've always wanted to do that you haven't done already.

3. From your list, pick one item and commit to doing it by next year.

"Fear keeps us focused on the past or worried about the future. If we can acknowledge our fear, we can realize that right now we are okay. Right now, today we are still alive, and our bodies are working marvelously. Our eyes can still see the beautiful sky. Our ears can still hear the voices of our loved ones."

~Thich Nhat Hanh

CHAPTER 7

DON'T ALLOW FEAR TO CONQUER

In a season where we as single ladies are trying to embrace who we are and where we are in life, excuse my broken English, but ain't nobody got time for fear. Fear is one of the enemy's favorite weapons of attack and is frequently used in war because it's known to be a liar and a thief. Where there is fear, there is no room for faith. One of my favorite Bible verses Philippians 4:6-7 tells us, "Don't worry about anything; instead, pray about everything. Tell God what you need, and thank Him for all He has done. Then you will experience God's peace, which exceeds anything we can understand. His peace will guard your hearts and minds as you live in Christ Jesus." This verse has gotten me through some tough times when I worried about my present and feared my future. When I first read this verse, it irked my soul, I thought to myself, *Yeah this is cute and all, but it's easier said than done to not worry about anything but pray.* Sometimes it's hard to just pray when you're in the thick of your storm. When things are not going according to your plan it's easy to allow fear and doubt to take over your mind.

Prayer sometimes seems like it takes too long because it doesn't work on our timeline, but consistent prayer and faith will change your outcome and perspective. It took a lot of praying and mental conditioning for me to begin to understand that eventually everything works together for my good. If I can have a little faith and weather the storm, then I will get through whatever life throws at me. You will never get rid of fear completely because there will always be a new challenge that will tests your faith, but you can choose to overcome it when it approaches and not let it consume your life. Fear robs many areas of our life including our perspective, our peace, time, purpose and blessings.

Fear Robs Your Perspective

Having a positive perspective is imperative in embracing your season of singleness. Perspective of seeing the glass half full as opposed to seeing it as half empty can change your view of any situation in your life. In situations where you may not be where you want to be in life, fear will kick in and have you anxious and worried that your circumstances are worse off than they are. Fear can convince a single woman who has many things going for her, and should be living life to the fullest, that because she is single her life is incomplete. You are what you tell yourself. A negative perspective doesn't change your situation it only makes you miserable while you're living it.

Fear Robs Your Peace

Along with stealing your perspective, fear will also steal your joy. There is joy in the little things in our life.

Spending time with loved ones, beautiful weather, great health, being able to laugh, being in your right mind without a mental illness, are all things that many of us have to be thankful for. If you have clothes on your back, food in your stomach, or transportation, you're blessed beyond belief. Worrying about the unknown, stressing about the future, or anxiety about things we can't change assassinates your peace. Peace in your life keeps you calm, thankful and sane. My father passed away suddenly a few years ago, and it was a devastating experience for me. He was only 56 years old and although he had health issues, no one really saw it coming. After his death, I had so much anxiety and worry about people dying in my family, especially my mother, that it started to consume my daily thoughts. The fear kept me up at night, if I called my mother and she didn't answer immediately, I would go into full panic, sometimes crying uncontrollably. If I found out a family member or friend was ill, I would immediately be overcome with dread and fear that I would lose them. I finally had to pray and ask God to remove that burden from me. I came to the realization that everyone will die, there is no way around it. I've lost grandparents, uncles, cousins, and a parent and although the grief hurt me, I survived and eventually healed. Instead of fearing when they would pass away I decided to create memories with as many of my loved ones as I can while they were still here. Your peace is priceless and you can't afford to allow anything or anyone to infiltrate it.

Fear Robs You of Your Time

Fear robs you of time by wasting it. The fear you have to start that new business venture, further your education, or joining in that ministry in which you're called to serve is wasting valuable time. If you sit and daydream about what you wish you could be instead of going after the things you want, you will look up and ten years will have passed. Once enough time has passed, fear will then convince you that you're too old to go after your dreams.

Wasted time will almost always end in regret. If there is something that you've always wanted to do in life; lose weight, travel the world, execute a vision, the time to prepare and go after what you want is today. Don't allow fear to have another second of your life. The clock is ticking.

Fear Robs Your Purpose

Your purpose gives your life meaning. Your purpose gives you an understanding of why God created you in the first place. You're here to leave your unique stamp on the world. Your purpose, whatever that may be is meant to inspire, influence, save, and ignite not just you, but the world you live in. God has put talents and gifts inside of you that are supposed to take you on a journey to learn them, perfect them, and ultimately use them for his people and Kingdom. Fear is a great tool of attack because fear will lead you to believe that you don't have the resources to live in your purpose, you're not smart enough, you're not qualified, your past is too dark, or people won't support you.

As I'm writing this book, I have no idea financially how I'm going to self-publish it. I don't have experience as a publisher, and I've never written professionally. Fear has crept in my mind every step during the process of this book, telling me that I don't have the resources to publish this book; I'm not qualified to write this book, my testimony is not big enough to change lives. But if you are reading this book, then I have proof that the devil is a liar and fear didn't defeat me. If your calling scares the living daylights out of you and achieving your goals seems near impossible, then you are on the right track. Your dreams and goals should be so big that you need faith and God to help you accomplish them. As the young people say, "shoot your shot." There's a chance you may miss your mark, but what if you don't? What if instead of failing, you succeed? What if even your failures are not actually failures, but minor setbacks that will prepare you for the win? You will miss 100% of the shots you don't take.

Fear Robs Your Blessings

Fear robs you of your blessings by blocking them. Dreams you're too fearful to chase will block the blessings of seeing your vision come to pass. Fear or worrying about what will happen in the future will block the blessing of enjoying your now. Fear of rejection, fear of not being accepted and loved, or anything else you can think of will immediately bring your blessings to a screeching halt. You are not living your life in abundance if you're ruled by fear. Pray, constantly bombard yourself with positive energy, and begin to train your mind to overcome the spirit of fear. Step out on faith.

JOURNALING TOPICS

1. Name a time when you allowed fear to do the following:

   a. Rob you of your peace

   b. Rob you of your time

   c. Rob you of your blessings

"No one can make you feel inferior

without your consent."

~ Eleanor Roosevelt

CHAPTER 8

KNOW YOUR WORTH

I'm a big football fan. Besides reading and writing
it's probably one of my favorite past times. Player contract
negotiations are one of the most interesting off the field
parts of the game. When the star player's contract is up,
he and his agent negotiate for a new contract with the
team. Sometimes the negotiations go smoothly where the
player is happy and the team is happy. Other times, the
player ends up getting traded to another team or sits out
team activities because he is not happy with what the
organization is offering him. This is where it gets good to
me. I'm usually rooting for the player to get the contract
that he wants because oftentimes what the player is
asking for is in line with what other players of his caliber
are being paid. As much as we know the players make,

the owners are making much more for doing not nearly as much of the work. It reminds me of another system way back when, but that's a topic for another book. The funny part of this is when that player threatens to hold out; many of the fans immediately turn on the star player. They send them nasty tweets and messages on social media, call them greedy, tell them they are millionaires and they should just be happy. This always confuses me because most people I know don't think they get paid enough so how can you get mad at a person who feels they deserve more but is being short changed. Think about how it makes you feel when someone doesn't appreciate your worth in the workplace or when someone doesn't appreciate your worth in your personal life?

Once you know your worth, don't negotiate. If you put in the work to be your best why settle for getting paid below average or below your worth? This applies to every aspect of our lives; when I say being paid I'm not just talking about money. Everything in this world costs something. If it doesn't cost money, it either costs time, energy, effort, respect, patience or growth. You must know your worth and what you offer. Be confident in what you bring to the team and if the team doesn't want to pay you your worth, be willing to sit out or go to a different team. Don't waste your time playing on a team that doesn't see your value.

No ladies, I'm not speaking of being a gold digger and measuring your value in terms of money. You're worth more than money can buy. You deserve someone to spend their energy on you, their effort on you, respect you, be patient with you and grow for you. If they can't do those things then they can't afford you. Someone who is not willing to invest their efforts in you doesn't determine your worth. People will try to convince you that you are worth less simply because they can't afford you. That's why you have to stay firm in knowing your worth. Don't be a flea market seller. A flea market seller negotiates with the buyer, often getting much less than the original asking price in desperation to make a sale. As soon as the consumer states that their price is too high or they can't afford the item, the flea market seller starts going lower on the price. You're not a flea market seller, you're a star player. Believe it and declare it! If you don't believe you're a star player, look into why you feel this way. What things do you feel you are lacking or missing in your life that keeps you from being a star player? Write down those things that you are struggling with. Now cross out all the things you can't control (i.e. skin color, disabilities, and your past mistakes). Now if there anything still on your list after you cross out the things you can't control or change, change the ones you can and boom just like that you're star.

Not negotiating your worth is not the same thing as being stubborn, contrary, inflexible or uncompromising. You must decide what values and morals that you won't compromise. If it makes you compromise your beliefs and ethics, they should be on the non-negotiable list.

I've struggle with compromising my worth when dating. I have compromised who I am, gone against things that I know weren't right for me and allowed people to waste my time all in an attempt to keep a relationship or friendship together. I've allowed people to give me half their effort, even though they were receiving all of mine, I given my body and time to a person who didn't value me and had no plans of being in my life long-term. Compromising my standards and beliefs and allowing someone to devalue me didn't get me any closer to my goal of having a healthy relationship that led to marriage, and I felt like crap when it was over. I vowed to myself that the last guy I dated would be the last time that I would allow someone in my space who didn't know my worth. I spent time after that relationship ended determining what things I needed to work on and work through. I rededicated my life to God, where I began to learn and believe his promises on my life and what truly made me beautiful. On my journey, I've met new spiritual friends, begun to learn and walk in my purpose, removed toxic behaviors and people from my life and replaced them with positivity and growth. I've been told all my life to know my worth and love myself, but I had to grow and get rid of some of my own baggage before I could truly see my worth. I decided that I will value myself and I will wait for what God has for me. As I grow and mature every day, I learn who I am and I what I truly want out a life.

Now that I know my worth and becoming the woman I want to be, I desire a man who loves and fears the Lord. I will not marry someone who does not serve the Lord. I will not date someone who refuses to respect me, who only texts, but never calls or only calls late at night. I won't entertain someone who is in another relationship. I don't want anyone else's man, I want my own. I will not tolerate someone who is physically, verbally, or emotional abusive. I want a man with ambition who doesn't want me to take care of him financially. In order to get to know me, it will take time and effort. You will actually have to hold a mature conversation about where you see yourself in 3-10 years. You won't be able to leave me in limbo about what we are. You don't get to waste my time. I will only accept being treated like a lady, not a home girl, not a side chick.

This is my price and it's not up for discussion. I may compromise on my political views, I may be open to try different food, listen to different music, but I'm not compromising on how I should be treated. Determine your value and don't offer discounts.

JOURNALING TOPICS

1. How have you dealt with people who didn't know your worth?

2. Are you currently involved in a situation where you're not being valued (i.e. relationship, job, or partnership)?

3. If you answered yes to number two, what steps can you to get out of that situation?

"But the LORD said to Samuel, 'Don't judge by his appearance or height, for I have rejected him. For the LORD doesn't see things the way you see them. People judge by outward appearance, but the Lord looks at the heart."

-1 Samuel 16:7 (NLT)

CHAPTER 9

STANDARDS

I stand behind that fact there are certain standards you shouldn't compromise, but there is a thin line. There is a difference between having self-respect, knowing your worth, and looking for someone equally yoked versus being superficial, unreasonable, unrealistic and closed minded. I won't go as far as saying some of our standards are too high, but I've known women—myself included—who may not have given a man a fair chance or they've had expectations for a potential man that even they don't possess.

If you've been single for a while, somewhere down the line, I'm sure someone has told you that you're just too picky. Take that label with a grain of salt because some people think that if you've been single for a while you should be open to date any and everyone just to say you're in a relationship. Think long and hard about your ideal mate and what good qualities you would like to see in them. I would recommend making a list. If you haven't noticed by now I really like list. If you decided to make a list, put a star by all the qualities that are extremely important to you that your mate has. Lastly circle all the items on your list that are absolutely non-negotiable qualities of a mate. Access your list and determine how many items you considered non-negotiable. I hope some of the things high on your list were character, there spiritual relationship with God, how they treat other people, how they respond to adversity, and goal orientated.

A person's character, behaviors, patterns, and actions should be closely analyzed in a potential mate. Looks fade, finances change, cars and jewelry go out of style and depreciate. You've seen enough recent pictures of your high school classmates on Facebook to know that looks are not forever. Being physically attracted to someone is important, but be careful of eliminating someone solely on the fact that they're not a ten in your eyes. You could be overlooking a true gem. Often times women especially can overlook appearances in exchange for being treated a certain way. I will take a God-fearing man, who is driven, has integrity and respect for women, over someone who's fine as Idris Elba, but irresponsible with no substance or plan for the future. Just like looks, money can fade as well. People may start off with a great financial picture, but they can lose their job, make a bad investment, or mismanage the money they have. Then you have those who look like money, but once you dig deeper everything they have is simply to impress others. They want to look rich instead of actually achieving financial stability. They are concerned with now and not concerned with their future.

Focus on getting to know someone and where they are going not necessarily where they are right now. A reliable glimpse into their future is their faith, attitude, ethics, and endurance.

I have a few friends who are the happily married and I remember being around when they could barely stand the sight of their future husbands. They were either too short, or annoying, or not their type or they didn't like the way the dressed, or they weren't cool enough or any other juvenile reason you could think of. Slowly but surely, they showed them what type of men they were and the next thing I know, I'm a bridesmaids in their weddings, play auntie of children, and celebrating anniversaries year after year. Pull back the physical layer and see what's underneath. You may be pleasantly surprised at what you find when you are a little open-minded. What's for you may be completely different than you ever imagined.

Your standards may be also getting in the way if you are comparing potential prospects to other people. Whether it be your ex, the fantasy guy you read about in your romance novels, your father, or someone else's man, comparisons are mental traps that ruin us every day. Comparisons are unrealistic once you dig deeper.

If you are looking for a man who has great character, strong faith, and a bright future, you should first make sure that you yourself provide those same qualities. There is no one out of your league, but some people are at a level of growth in their lives that will require you to elevate yourself in order for a relationship with them to work Get you faith, money, and spirit up so you can walk into a room with your head held high knowing that you are becoming God intended you to be. Take some time to reevaluate your standards and analyze if they are realistic. Ensure that your expectations are fair and open to compromise. Don't block the chance to get to know a beautiful soul.

JOURNALING TOPICS

1. Make a list of 10 traits that you would like in a significant other

2. How many of those traits are negotiable and how many are non-negotiable?

3. How many things are related to physical appearances?

"In creating you, God has already given you everything you need to live a life of endurance, abundance, and purpose."

~Brandy Lucas

CHAPTER 10

SINGLE, NOT INCOMPLETE

Life is about constantly growing and overcoming. It doesn't make you less than because you struggle in certain areas and need some work. Take it one day and one item off your list at a time. Begin with the things that you can control and pray on the rest. Start to speak positivity in your life daily and most importantly, take action. Go head girl and write that book, go sky diving, go back to school, or buy that house yourself. Do what you always wanted to do in life with no fear. Don't wait on love, don't wait on reassurance, just enjoy your season, because like all seasons, it will change.

When you do find love and marriage, you will be confident in who you are and what you stand for. You won't settle out of fear of being alone because you overcame that demon. You will say, hey I grew to like being alone so if I have to go back, I will survive. Love yourself enough to wait for what is for you. Don't be anxious about the future and don't regret the past. Learn to live in peace and love. Once you start to master these concepts, you will have a glow about you and you will attract what you are. Anyone that comes into your life will be an addition, not a completion. Become the woman striving to be the best version of herself, not the woman grabbing pieces of someone else in an attempt to fill the voids in her life.

If you're not there yet, fake it until you make. Keep reciting affirmations to yourself until you believe it. Just like running a marathon, you have to train your body over a long period of time to be able to run 26-plus miles. The same thing holds true with your mind, if you train your mind to think positive it will. If you remove toxic thoughts, people and energy long enough, your outlook on life will change. If you pray for peace and tell yourself great things about yourself, your self-esteem will improve and stress levels will decrease. Bad days will still come but they won't destroy you when they do. Make room for victories, don't let anything steal your joy and have faith! The next time you feel anxiety, fear, or incomplete because you're single, remember you're a star player, and you're single, not dead.

GOODREADS & AMAZON REVIEWS

ARE GREATLY APPRECIATED.

STAY CONNECTED!

INSTAGRAM: @singlenotdead

TWITTER: @single_notdead

FACEBOOK: brandylucastheauthor

WEBSITE: www.brandylucas.com

EMAIL: brandy@brandylucas.com

www.ingramcontent.com/pod-product-compliance
Lightning Source LLC
Chambersburg PA
CBHW070809050426
42452CB00011B/1957